# Above All, BE GOOD

## The Story of the Stoics and their Teachings

Cover Image: Wikimedia Commons contributors, «File:Temple of Portunus - Rome.JPG,» Wikimedia Commons, https://commons.wikimedia.org/w/index.php?title=File:Temple_of_Portunus_-_Rome.JPG&oldid=317410033 (accessed October 18, 2019).

Edited & Designed by New Acropolis Cultural Organization (Mumbai, India)

Published in 2019 by

NEW ACROPOLIS

New Acropolis Cultural Organization.
Mumbai, India.
www.acropolis.org.in
info@acropolis.org.in



ISBN: 978-81-920193-7-6

Printed in India.

# CONTENTS

# PREFACE

This book does not aim to be an academic treatise on Stoicism.

I'm not a professional philosopher. I'm simply a lover of wisdom, a Philosophos - a person who is intrigued by, and attracted to, the mysteries of life, and is inspired by those who came before me and their own inner and outer investigations into the nature of reality.

I study philosophy in a modern school of philosophy in the classical style, and have been blessed in encountering inspiring individuals, who I dare to call my teachers, and who have guided me in this philosophical path.

In that sense I believe I'm in good company, as many of the philosophers of the past, from Plato to Marcus Aurelius, studied philosophy in the classical manner, and transmitted it from one practitioner to another, from teacher to disciple.

As a musician, I find that philosophy and music have much in common, as both can be approached from a solely theoretical perspective or from an aspiration to create, to realize, to LIVE under the guidance of the great role models of the past.

Therefore, while my theoretical knowledge of the Stoics may be limited, I have experimented with their practices, and have found in them a great source of wisdom and counsel.

In this book I have tried to give some historical background and theoretical insight into the ideas of the Stoics, not aiming for it to be a complete review, as this would require a hefty tome, and would miss the intention of this small treatise. For me, the story of the Stoics is just an excuse to transmit their teachings and the teachings of their companions to a new generation which is facing great trials, and may find help perhaps in the wisdom of the ancients.

While the Stoic doctrine is imperfect, it is still a wonderful source of wisdom for today's world in crisis, a resource that any eclectic seeker of wisdom will benefit from tremendously.

# PART I

# INTRODUCTION: STOICISM IN OUR TIMES

# WHO WERE THE STOICS?

Stoicism was a school of thought and action formed by a continuous chain of teachers and disciples who lived around the beginning of the first millennium, seeking and living, through investigation and practice, the answer for the age old philosophical question: how to live the good life?

We all want to live a good life, but while most of us receive the ready-made answers offered by our education, media and friends, the Stoics, like other classical philosophy schools, believed that the real answer to this question must pass through the use of our own reason, that enigmatic part of ourselves, the only part of ourselves that can contemplate itself and all the parts of our being.

Today, when we wish to study martial arts or music, we seek a teacher, a person who can use her or his experience to accelerate our progress, to point out possible pitfalls, and with the best teachers, to initiate us into the mysteries of the discipline. Most people would not study with someone who learned Tai-Chi or Aikido from YouTube videos. They seek a person who has studied with a Master, who himself has studied with his own master, and so on.

For the Stoics, living was an art, the highest of them all. And if we study the various arts with a teacher, then all the more reason to do so with the art of living. Living well is therefore a subject of study that requires the example and instruction of a proficient teacher, a person who has made evident progress in the subject matter. Therefore, Stoicism was a school of teachers and disciples, whose teaching was nothing other than life itself.

Stoicism was not a dead academic subject or religious dogma, but a living and evolving discipline, continuously refined and enriched by the everyday experiences, writings and teachings of contemporary Stoics of the time. The sharing and transmission of Stoicism was an essential part of the Stoic life - from teacher to disciple, and from one comrade on the path to the other. This transmission of ideas, insights and experience, allowed Stoicism to develop and prosper for five hundred years. It began in 301BC, when the young Zeno of Citium began teaching his first students at the painted colonnade (Stoa) of Athens, and reached its apex with Marcus Aurelius, serving as a guiding force to the emperor who ruled the Roman empire for 19 years (161 – 180AD).

Today, in an age of "going with what you feel" and "living the moment", it is no wonder that Stoicism has acquired a bad name for itself, one of indifference and lack of emotionality. But Stoicism is not about indifference; it is about realizing that our emotions are not always the best judges of situations or people, so we need to seek a more objective means to make better decisions in life. Objective does not mean robotic or inhumane. On the contrary, to be objective means to put our own subjective opinion in the context of a wider point of view, in aspiration of the greater good, taking into consideration all the possible factors, including the feelings of those around us.

Many evil things have been done in the name of the greater good. That is why LOVE is a crucial element in the philosophical process, without which we lose sight of the right means, and even if our goal is noble, it becomes sour with cruelty and indifference.

Every sub-culture and society envisions and crowns its ideal human being. For some of us, the ideal human being is the "celebrity" or the hi-tech genius and entrepreneur.

For the Stoics, the ideal person was the sage, a person who is wise, tranquil, indifferent to external achievements, and is content and happy through the practice of virtue. As the sage was an ideal figure, none of the Stoics admitted to being one. However, this image of the sage became an archetype to aspire and progress towards, throughout life. Today, we can find the figure of the Sage reflected in the modern mythological figures of Yoda, Morpheus and Gandalf.

The sage is naturally also the ideal politician, since the best politician is the one who serves his people without self-interest. Self-interest is the enemy of justice, which requires a certain level of detachment and objectivity, and no personal involvement.

For the Stoics the good life was intrinsically linked to freedom. Their concept of freedom, however, was a controversial one. For them, freedom is not attained through the satisfaction of desires, but through the sublimation of desires.

Stoicism reached its apex in the 2nd century, with the reign of the "five good emperors", a time in which the historian Gibbon claimed "the condition of the human race was the most happy". These five good emperors - Nerva, Trajan, Hadrian, Antonius Pius and especially Marcus Aurelius - were all inspired by or practitioners of Stoic philosophy and good examples of what can happen when moral philosophy unites with politics.

Ironically, with Commodus, the son of Marcus Aurelius (the only biological son to inherit the empire in 100 years), begins the "Crisis of the 3rd century" which led to the dying gasps of the Roman Empire, its formal acceptance of the Christian faith and its eventual fall.

There are times in the cyclical history of humanity when humanity goes through a period of disconnection and forgetfulness, when there is no direction and the individual is lost and tends to live only for the sake of survival. At these times morality becomes an option and a rarity. What used to be a common act of courtesy, becomes a news item, and what used to be a shocking news item, becomes a common occurrence.

In times like these, organized religion and politics are not trusted and many feel they no longer offer a valid solution to the moral needs of man. In times like these, people need moral philosophers to give them a rational and structured path to morality, which is the collection of habits and behaviors that allow us to live a good, just and harmonious life.

## Philosophy in the Eyes of the Stoics

Today, the word philosophy is sometimes associated with lectures and books full of big and complicated words. It is seen as a curious but unnecessary field of study that entertains people with extra money and time, but has no practical value to everyday modern life.

To the ancient and classical schools of philosophy, however, philosophy was something else. It was a discipline, a way of life, a practical and gradual method aimed towards living the good life. Plato's Academics, the Pythagoreans, the Cynics, the Neoplatonists and the Stoics, would all be surprised by the view of philosophy we have today, as for them philosophy was an axis of being, a far cry from today's heavy books and complicated words.

Our society has made great achievements in the empirical and physical sciences, resulting in technological improvements. However, we are gradually discovering this is not enough. While these achievements can improve the means with which we live our lives, they do not bring us closer to answering the question of what is a good life, and more importantly, how to live it.

Before the birth of philosophy, people referred to the wisdom traditions to find these answers. These were the Mystery religions, in which the aspirant went through initiations through which he experienced the meaning of life through rites and symbols. When these traditions gradually decayed, philosophy as a public access point to wisdom, was born.

The stoics were not just theoretical thinkers. From Marcus Aurelius, who wasn't just a Roman emperor - the most powerful person in his world - but one of the best Roman emperors, to Epictetus, who began his life as a slave, and ended it a friend of emperor Hadrian, and one of the most respected citizens of the Roman world, the Stoics exemplified their doctrine through action, and did not shirk from their duties, whether in politics or any other spheres of life.

Today, the Stoics are experiencing a rebirth. Stoicism developed in times in which people were losing touch with metaphysical values and the wisdom of the ancients, and they could no longer find the answers they needed in decadent religions. Today, after the disintegration of the moral traditions of our cultures, we are seeking answers as well, a wise way of life in a chaotic world. Their pragmatic teachings find ready ears among contemporary seekers, as they come from a time very similar to our own.

# ABOVE ALL, BE GOOD

The Stoics were first of all a school of moral philosophy. Morality for the Stoics was not an adornment or a preference, but the central axis of their whole teachings. All their other techniques were meaningless without a moral purpose.

At these times of global crises, it is natural that the Stoics will resurface on the world stage offering viable and practical methods and techniques to confront the challenges of life, in all its aspects. Stoic principles are used today in fields as diverse as business and football.

With its very practical approach to life, it is easy to focus on the techniques aimed at promoting individual and commercial goals. The teachings of philosophy are accessible and useful for all, and in all fields of life.

However, when we transfer ideas from the past to the present, we always risk disfiguring the ideas, in order to fit them into our cultural and mental box.

We all live in a certain moral ecology, a cultural and mental "aquarium" - the norms and mental patterns proper to our space and time. These are things we take for granted because we have been born into them, and have never confronted them with other ideas. Einstein said, "What knows a fish about water?" And all of us are fish in the aquarium of our preconceptions and prejudices. For example, the idea of property – my house, my stuff, my land, etc. - was so prevalent in the European way of thinking, that when they came to the "New World" it was hard for them to imagine or understand the completely different view of the Native Americans.

In the same way, when we invoke the Stoics from their world – The Mediterranean basin at the turn of the first millennium – we naturally tend to choose the parts we want and cut off whatever doesn't fit into our mentality. For example, as material and personal achievement is a prevalent goal in our society, we may take the Stoic ideas that can help us achieve these goals, and neglect others, which may be of even more important value.

This is mostly harmless but can also lead to dangerous misinterpretations.

For example, one powerful idea that Epictetus presents is: to turn every circumstance to one's advantage. On the one hand, this can be interpreted as using every obstacle as a chance for growth, transcending our limitations, and to practice detachment. Or it can be interpreted in a Machiavellian sense: to turn every situation into an opportunity for personal gain. This second interpretation is completely against the ethical stand of the Stoics, and the opposite of its original intention. While the Stoics were politicians, they were never schemers. And this can be seen clearly in *Meditations*. In the spirit of Socrates, it is better to suffer injustice than to cause one. Above all, be good.

Another example is the Stoics' commitment to community service and their sense of responsibility towards humanity. Our culture of competition and excessive individualism puts us in a constant pursuit of self-promotion, trying to get ahead of the rest, and to "sell" ourselves and what we do. While we feel this may be necessary for survival, it can also mislead us into empowering our identification with our Ego, constantly pushing ourselves forward and seeking personal gain.

Therefore, we cannot forget the essence of the Stoic teachings - its moral and ethical message. It is THE essence of their teachings.

If we use the techniques of the Stoics, leaving the moral aspect to second or last place, we would be unfaithful to the beautiful heritage the Stoics left to us. Moreover, the moral message of the Stoics is their most important and useful.

Inspired by the Stoic teachings, we can develop wonderful qualities, such as discipline, detachment and firmness. But without the heart of the teachings, we can direct these qualities only towards our personal and, why not, selfish goals. Stoicism does not go well with greed, deceit, self-aggrandizement and manipulation, no matter how "successful" they make us.

For the Stoics, as well as for other classical philosophers, the good and the bad are not found in our circumstances, but in our own reactions to our circumstances. If we follow our conscience and reason and act ethically, we are doing good. If we act unethically, we are doing bad, and we harm our soul. The rest is indifferent, that is, inessential. Success is not measured in external achievements, but in internal conquests.

Every pleasant and convenient thing can be a 'positive indifferent', as long as we are able to maintain our moral axis in achieving it. Every unpleasant and inconvenient thing can be a 'negative indifferent' to be avoided, as long as we are able to maintain our moral axis in avoiding it.

A successful career, for example, can be a nice thing to have, so long as we don't sacrifice our principles for it. Unemployment sucks, but if we have to choose it to maintain our ethics, then it is good. Whether we have a job or not is not the essential thing, but whether we have an ethical backbone is. Of course, to have a job is preferable to not having a job, as it helps us take care of our responsibilities.

This turns our focus from external accomplishments, to the everyday dilemmas of each moment. How am I taking responsibility over this moment? How am I fulfilling my duty to myself and to humanity at each moment? Am I living fully and responsibly?

These are grounding questions that connect the macrocosmos with the microcosmos, and bring us to the present moment.

## Stoicism and Social Responsibility

It is clear that humanity today is going through a crisis. The visible aspects of this crisis are seen on the economic, environmental, political and cultural levels, among many others. But at its root, this crisis is neither ecological nor economical, but moral. All these different aspects reflect the same hidden cause. This crisis begins in the heart of man, and that is where it will end.

Let's ask ourselves, why do we have ecological and economic problems? Why do we have wars and conflicts? How long will the wars on drugs, poverty, hunger and war itself, continue, until we realize we're approaching it the wrong way?

Some say it's a god given reality. But as far as I am able to tell, God doesn't tell anybody what to do. These situations are a result of greed, apathy and even laziness, and these are all found in the human psyche. So this is not divine intervention, but just our own human faults and weaknesses.

When we don't like the content of a television show, we don't call a technician to fix the TV set. But on a social level, this is what usually happens. Instead of fixing the cause, we try to reform this or that program, make or cancel regulations, change this or that administrator. But when the TV show is bad, what you want to do is to change the content, not fix the TV.

In the human sphere, the content is found in the inner world – the psychological, ethical and spiritual spheres. While the spiritual may be beyond our reach, in the sense that we cannot affect it, we must work in the ethical sphere, which is the reflection of the spiritual in our everyday actions.

From the early days of the Roman Empire, the Stoics formed

a resistance to tyranny and corruption, but this resistance was not as much against the tyrant personally, as it was an inner resistance against oneself engaging in any unethical actions, or neglecting one's duty.

Epictetus writes: "*When Vespasian sent for Helvidius Priscus and commanded him not to go into the Senate, he replied, 'It is in your power not to allow me to be a member of the Senate, but so long as I am, I must go in.' 'Well, go in then,' says the emperor, 'but say nothing.' 'Do not ask my opinion, and I will be silent.' 'But I must ask your opinion.' 'And I must say what I think right.' 'But if you do, I shall put you to death.' 'When then did I tell you that I am immortal? You will do your part, and I will do mine: it is your part to kill; it is mine to die, but not in fear: yours to banish me; mine to depart without sorrow.'" (Discourses, 1.2.19-21)*

This is a wonderful example of an impersonal stoic resistance. We cannot control the actions of others, especially the powers that be, but we can definitely control our own, and make our own choices, taking into consideration whatever consequences they may have.

This is highly relevant in today's political atmosphere, which very much revolves around the personalities of politicians, and not around ideas. To attack personalities, is not only undignified, but it is also useless. Instead the Stoics offer a much more reasonable form of resistance, based on one's own initiative and actions – *in my own sphere of influence, I choose to take responsible and conscious actions, and not to go against my conscience.*

We cannot control the greed of corporations, yet we can control our own greed, our own constant desire for more than we need, which feeds the greed of the corporations. A charlatan or snake oil salesman can only succeed if they have gullible clients who wish to find magical and easy cures for their conditions. There will always be ignorant predators, ignorant for not seeing the bigger consequences of their actions, but whether they succeed or not depends on whether we are willing to be ignorant prey.

Therefore, the change cannot start from without; it must start within every one of us. Because we don't have control over the external circumstances, only on our own selves.

When speaking about the Stoics it's easy to focus on emotional and mental control, on duty, on finding solutions to the challenges of our lives, but we shouldn't forget that above all the Stoics were good people, or at least aspired to be. This is something we don't need to over analyze. Marcus Aurelius wrote, "don't discuss too much what it means to be a good person, just be one".

This ethical-moral axis cannot be overemphasized. Stoicism is a rational and practical method which can be used to improve ourselves in all aspects of life. But, this aspect of Stoicism, the central idea of goodness, is sometimes conveniently underestimated by contemporary writers. Why? Because it means the Stoics didn't aim just for personal happiness or success. The word success in fact doesn't appear once in the writings of Marcus Aurelius.

The important thing is to fulfill our duties in the best way and to be good people. We are the ones who need to climb upwards to reach their lofty ideals, and not to lower them down to us.

Epictetus tells us that we should never miss an opportunity to help a friend in need. Don't let the thoughts of your lower mind, the constant gain-calculator, to prevent you from being helpful.

"What are my duties?" was the question every Stoic asked himself, and a question each of us needs to ask ourselves. According to the Stoics we all have duties in life, some larger, some smaller, but each of us must take care to fulfill our duties in the best way possible, whether as citizens, family men, friends, teachers or leaders.

Stoicism is a philosophy of taking part, of responsibility and commitment – words that may scare some, until we understand that they are synonymous to purpose and sense of meaning. Within us, we all want to take part in something, to be a part of something which is greater than ourselves, and that gives meaning to our existence.

The ideals of Stoicism do not belong to the Stoics. We find them resonating strongly among the Samurai in Japan, as well as among the warrior tribes of indigenous North America such as the Lakota and the Apachee. They characterize a way of life that emerges and is reborn with the cycles of history and under different guises in different cultures and places. It is an aspect of the human experience, it is the way of life of the INNER WARRIOR.

# PART II

# THE TRANSMISSION OF WISDOM

## THE STORY OF THE STOICS

Ideas pass through the ages like fire, from torch to torch, from one burning lamp to another. Sometimes they are held aloft to shine brightly for all, and sometimes they are like burning embers, passing secretly through trembling hands. Sometimes they are transmitted formally, in an organized manner, and at times they are transmitted by stragglers on the path, individuals who do their best to keep the fire going. Yet, as long as there is one source still aflame, it can give new life to the ancient beacons and give light to many lamps.

Ideas are transmitted through words, through images, through sounds and music. There is no end to the creativity of mankind.

Stoicism as a set of ideas, which formed an aspect of the Classical wisdom tradition, appears clearly on the pages of history for six hundred years, initially transmitted as part of the formal Stoic school and later by a continuous, yet probably unformalized, series of teachers and disciples. After the death of Marcus Aurelius and the setting of the Dark Ages, it resurges periodically above the waters of history as thinkers and philosophers go back to its sources for new inspiration, but never has it experienced a return to its golden age as in the Roman Empire.

In its journey through time, the branchlet of Stoicism has merged, separated from, and rejoined other currents of the great river of Philosophy, which flows continuously towards Sophia, the sea of wisdom. Nevertheless, it mostly kept its own unique color and nature, enough to be able to track its students and adherents back in time.

We know these philosophers as icons, but they were human beings just like us, with personal challenges and doubts, with loves and failures, with victories and with sacrifices.

Put yourselves in the boots of Aristocles of Athens, better known today by the name of "Plato" (wide shoulders) a nickname given to him by his wrestling coach. A young man with an affinity for writing and poetry, from a well-to-do family, whose parents obviously wanted him to continue in their political and legal family line. But then he encounters the inspiring figure of Socrates, who some see as a fringe character, a "gadfly" who keeps bothering people with his intimate questions. Yet this "gadfly" awakens him to the seeking of wisdom, and inspires him to dedicate his youth to philosophy.

Imagine witnessing the people of your beloved city voting to put your beloved teacher to death for some racked up charges of "blasphemy" and "corrupting the youth", made by political enemies, the feeling... of injustice and the growing aspiration to form a better, more just society.

Imagine traveling throughout Italy and sailing to the mysterious and wonderful land of Egypt, where the last initiation centers preserve knowledge from primeval times, where you go through unforgettable experiences of soul and spirit.

Imagine coming back to your homeland and establishing a school for young people with inquietudes, like you, and imagine bringing your teacher back to life through your writings, to be used as study materials for your beloved young disciples.

Every true philosopher today is a disciple of Plato, of Socrates, of Zeno and Epictetus. Who knows? Perhaps you could BE the Zeno or Epictetus of our times.

In this chapter we will attempt to give a brief review of the main characters in this story of transmission, not for the sake of historical research, but in order to see ourselves in these heroic pioneers of a way of life. What we wish to emphasize is the example and teachings given by the lives of these great philosophers.

## The Early Stoa

(The 7 Original Scholarchs)

## The Middle Stoa

(The official Stoic school falls apart and the transition to Rome)

## The Late Stoa

(The Philosophy of Emperors)

|  |  |  |
|---|---|---|
| Founder of Stoicism | 334-262BC | **Zeno of Citium** |
| | 330-230BC | **Cleanthes** |
| The 2nd Founder of Stoicism | 279-206BC | **Chryssipus of Soli** |
| | | **Zeno of Tarsus** |
| The First Stoic in Rome | 230BC-140/150BC | **Diogenes of Babylon** |
| | died 130BC | **Antipater of Tarsus** |
| The Bridge to a New World | 185BC-110BC | **Panaetius** |

|  |  |  |
|---|---|---|
| Educating the Roman Nobility | 185BC–110BC | **Panaetius** |
| | 160-85BC | **Mnesarchus** |
| | 160-85BC | **Dardanus** |
| Rome | 95-46BC | **Cato the Younger** |
| The Roman Eclectic | 106-43BC | **Cicero** |

|  |  |  |
|---|---|---|
| The Emperor's Teacher | 4BC – 65AD | **Seneca the Younger** |
| | 35-118AD | **Euphrates the Stoic** |
| The Teacher | 1st century AD | **Musonius Rufus** |
| The Philosopher of Freedom | 55-135AD | **Epictetus** |
| | c. 86/89 – c. after 146/160AD | **Arrian of Nicomedia** |
| The Five Good Emperors | 100-170AD | **Quintus Junius Rusticus** |
| The Philosopher-Emperor | 121-180AD | **Marcus Aurelius** |

# THE EARLY STOA

In order to understand what life was like in the time of the Early Stoa we need to exercise our imagination. It is difficult for us to truly understand historical events, and to put ourselves in the shoes of the human beings who preceded us in this world.

In one paragraph, historians can write about macro-processes of tens and hundreds of years, which were experienced by several generations of human beings. But the individual who lived at that time did not experience an historical process, but only his or her own daily life, with its joys and challenges, affected by large scale historical movements, which are usually recognized only in the rear-view mirror.

We tend to think these people were very different from us. But underneath their strange customs and words, we find the human experience, which essentially has not changed that much.

We all have bodies, minds and emotions. We all live in a society and interact with people, some more harmoniously than others, and we all are trying to lead what we believe is a good life, to the best of our abilities, mostly fumbling in the darkness, but sometimes with the light of our intelligence and intuition.

Although there are no definite start and end points in the flow of history, we must choose a point to begin our story and there's no better place than the appearance of the singular figure of Socrates on the pages of history.

## Socrates (470 - 399BC)

Despite being one of the most familiar names in the history of philosophy, we in fact have very little concrete information about his life and his teachings. What we do know is that his depth and way of being attracted the most intelligent young minds of his city, and he made such an impact on them that most of the later philosophy schools in Greece and the Hellenistic world were founded by his disciples, or by disciples of his disciples.

Somehow, with his integral way of being, his haranguing questions, and above all with the example of his life, he lit a spark of inner movement and transformation that impelled those who were able, to begin their own independent journey towards Truth, the highest philosophical aim.

As in many other times in history, those who make people think, are put down by those who don't want people to think. Through accusation of impiety and "corrupting" the youth, Socrates was sentenced to death by the Athenian democracy.

But a great teacher never dies. There is a clear and continuous chain connecting Socrates to Marcus Aurelius, a chain of many generations, and through this chain one message seems to radiate through - Above all, be good.

His teachings continued to reverberate through the various schools of philosophy founded by his spiritual descendants – among which are those who inspired the Stoic school – Plato, Antisthenes and Euclides, among others.

## Philosophy as a Way of Life - The Hellenic Schools of Philosophy

Socrates was only the spark, because after his death, his disciples and their followers formed their own schools of philosophy, among which were the Academics, Cynics, Pyrrhonists and others. While the details of their teachings varied from one school to another, they all shared several principles in common:

* Philosophy as a way of life – to be a philosopher is not just an intellectual pursuit but a realization of ideas in practice. The

philosopher is an example and proof of what he teaches, and not just a person who can debate with other philosophers or to share interesting ideas.

* Philosophy encompasses all areas of life – Philosophy is the love of wisdom, and therefore it is occupied with the diverse aspects of the human experience, ranging from the problems of family and occupation, to the sciences of music, mathematics and astronomy. Nothing is outside the scope of philosophy, it deepens, elevates and unifies every field of knowledge.

* Philosophy as a path to living the good life – while they had different approaches, the aim of these schools was common and practical. They aimed to answer the question of what is a good life, and to live the answer.

* Philosophy as a path to living in harmony with other people – these "schools" were formed by students from all walks of life, who shared classes and experiences together, and sometimes even lived together. They formed philosophical friendships based on their common pursuit which also allowed them to practice their aspired virtues.

## Diogenes and The Cynics

While visiting Corinth, Alexander the Great found Diogenes of Sinope in his usual abode, sitting in the street, enjoying the sunny day.

When asked by the ruler of the world if there is any favor he can do for him, Diogenes the cool replied in the affirmative: "Please move aside, you are blocking the sun." To that Alexander said: "If I were not Alexander, then I should wish to be Diogenes."

This story, whether true or not, reveals the archetypal ideal of the Cynic school of philosophy. This inner contentment, which raised even the envy of the most powerful, was the pursuit of this school of philosophy, and was later adopted by the Stoics.

What would we do if a powerful billionaire offered us a favor?

Would we have the inner contentment necessary to tell them we don't need anything?

Or do we feel that all our problems will be solved if only we could get a break? A raise? Win the lottery?

Self-sufficiency or Autarky - the freedom to be happy, regardless of the circumstances, is precisely the freedom sought by the Cynics, and later by the Stoics.

The idea that virtue by itself is enough for a complete life, that there's no need for the superfluous luxuries of civilization, has been brought to the extreme by Diogenes, who when seeing a boy using his hands to cup water from the fountain, broke his only possession, a bowl, saying that he now sees that he was carrying extra baggage with him all along. This practice was complemented by a complete disdain of social norms and taboos, including urinating on people and defecating in the theater, among other things. This as a protest against all social customs as artificial constructs.

Diogenes may not have been an example we would all wish to follow, but he was a man of ethical integrity, that is, he followed through with his principles to their logical end. He lived what he taught. He walked the talk. There was no inconsistency between his teachings and his life. And there is no better way to examine our principles than to live them as completely and thoroughly as we can. Either they will lead us to where we thought they would, or we will discover we need to rethink and readjust them.

Whether Diogenes felt his way of life brought him the good life he sought, we cannot say. But the fact that he chose to live in the city and not retire to some mountain cave, teaches us that he still found some purpose in social life, and that perhaps his behavior was extreme in order to make an impact, and not an aim in itself.

Like the Cynic, the Stoic practices **self-sufficiency,** or **Autarky** (αὐτάρκεια), with the belief that even the most powerful man in the world cannot give us happiness.

We find that "successful" people by society's standards may be miserable, while humble people can be full of joy, and vice versa. This teaches us that money, status, relationships, romance, etc., in and of themselves do not guarantee happiness.

Self-sufficiency means to seek happiness within ourselves, independent of external circumstances. Not to wait for that "one" person, or that dream job, because nobody and nothing can provide us with what we have already within us. It is the difficult understanding that nobody can solve our problems or to take our steps for us.

Another idea which may have inspired the first Stoics, was the idea of achieving **mental clarity,** or **Atufia** (ἀ-τυφια), which literally means not-fog (τύφος). The fog we are referring to is a type of *mind-fog* (coincidentally, the name of the typhus disease originates from this word, because of the mental state of those who carry this disease). This fog, like the fog that gathers on the front window of a car, does not let us see what's going on in front of our eyes.

What is this *mind-fog?* It is a state of mind characterized by haziness and mental numbness, which is created by false perceptions, mindlessness, uncontrolled passions, all leading to a state of mental blindness, that is, ignorance.

Cynicism became very popular with young people, but in time, like with many other schools of thought, a lot of these young people begin imitating the external aspects of their role models, in this case, austerity and shamelessness, without the depth of inner contemplation and the search for authentic insight, leading Epictetus to comment: "Consider the present Cynics who are dogs that wait at tables, and in no respect imitate the Cynics of old except perchance in breaking wind." *(Discourses, 3.22. 80)*

The Cynics are in the heart of every modern punk and anarchist. They, who don't want to change organized society, but see it as unnecessary and unnatural. While their approach doesn't offer a comprehensive and integral solution, we always need those who challenge the social norms, reminding us not to take them for granted, but to continuously review them for artificiality, pretense and obsolescence.

## ZENO OF CITIUM (c. 334 – c. 262 BC)
The First Stoic

*"Happiness is a good flow of life." (Zeno of Citium)*
Zeno of Citium is considered to be the first Stoic. He, however, did not consider himself a Stoic, but only a philosopher - a lover of wisdom.

Legend has it that a hundred years after the death of Socrates, Zeno found himself shipwrecked in Athens where in a small bookstore he found a book about the legendary philosopher. Impressed, he asked the owner where he might find someone like Socrates, and the owner immediately pointed to Crates, a famous cynic philosopher and disciple of Diogenes, who just happened to pass by.

**Zeno of Citium, National Archeological Museum, Naples (Italy). Roman copy of Greek original probably from 3rd century BC.** Sculptor unknown. Photo by Paulo Monti, 1969, Creative Commons License

Following Crates for a while, he was impressed by his dedication and courage. Being an eclectic philosopher, he was open to the various philosophical stances of his times, and did not reject an idea without considering it. To be eclectic does not mean to accept every idea, to be so open-minded that your brain slips out. But it does mean to consider every idea, without prejudice, dogmas or social pressure and with an authentic desire for truth. And once you recognize a truthful idea, to grab hold of it and begin to live accordingly. Eclecticism was always a rare trait, as we usually find it easier to cling to limiting definitions, and not follow the eclectic motto of finding truth wherever and from whomsoever it can be found.

We either follow blindly or reject blindly, instead of following consciously and rejecting intelligently.

Zeno took those ideas he found truthful and useful from Crates, but continued his search, studying with the Megarians and finally the Academicians who exposed him to Plato's ideas.

All three of these schools (Cynics, Megarians and Platonists) were formed by disciples of Socrates, and all of them were once again merged together by Zeno. Therefore, Zeno of Citium was in a way a spiritual great-grandson of Socrates.

After studying for some years with these different teachers, Zeno began teaching on his own, speaking to anyone who would listen, at the painted colonnade (Stoa) of the Agora of Athens, which is the reason his pupils, originally called Zenonians, became known as Stoics, or those who go to the Stoa.

One can imagine him pacing up and down, his words echoing among the columns and beautiful frescoes, surrounded by his eager and attentive disciples. Nevertheless, to be a disciple of Zeno was not an easy experience for the ego, as he was a strict teacher, saying for example to one overzealous youth, "We have one tongue and two ears, to listen twice as much as we speak."

While none of Zeno's writings have survived to our times, what we know from later Stoics tells us that the seeds of all the central principles of Stoicism were already laid by Zeno's teachings. There is also evidence of more esoteric writings that were not revealed to students, until they had proven themselves to be genuine philosophers. Be that as it may, from the first impulse given by Zeno, a formal school of philosophy was established, initiating a chain of teachers and disciples.

## CLEANTHES

The torch of Stoicism was passed from the hands of Zeno to his closest disciple Cleanthes, a former boxer, who carried water for a living.

Cleanthes wasn't a very successful individual in today's terms. In fact it is said he was so poor that he wrote Zeno's lectures on oyster shells and the blade bones of oxen, as he didn't have money to buy paper.

However, he did whatever he needed to do to continue his

philosophy studies with Zeno, whether he had to draw water or dig. He worked hard, but did so because he had a purpose in mind. His was the best career - a philosopher and a disciple of wisdom.

He wrote many books, on everything from the art of love, the laws and marriage, to politics and the gods. However, of his many writings very few survive, among which is the beautiful Hymn to Zeus.

Early Stoicism was still strongly influenced by Hellenismos, the ancient Greek religion, and its Archetypes. The hymn written by Cleanthes demonstrates the religious and mystical origins of Stoicism. These roots are somewhat forgotten because they don't resonate very well with our modern way of thinking, but they are fascinating to discover.

For the Stoics, as well as other philosophy schools, the Gods represented archetypes, principles of nature, and elements of the unknown. They were the powers working in the invisible, in immensely long time frames, activating processes we are unaware of and moving reality around (see below "Who are the Gods?").

Zeus in particular, was the representation of universal law. Law sets the boundaries, what can and can't be done, what is possible and impossible; it regulates the flow of life and directs it.

Cleanthes succeeded Zeno and acted as the scholarch of the Stoic school for more than 30 years, till the advanced age of 99.

Excerpts from the
**HYMN TO ZEUS**
**By Cleanthes**

*"Most Glorious and omnipotent Zeus, Ruler of Nature, **worshiped under many names**, by whom all things are governed in accordance to Law, hail to thee!*
*All things on earth, in the sea, or in the air confess thee as their*

*author, except the deeds of the evil and foolish;* ***but even such discords you know how to weave into a total harmony,*** *making what is disorderly orderly, what is hostile friendly, in accordance with* ***the Law of Reason which blind men cannot understand.***

***Instead they suffer loss when they seek happiness in their own fashion, knowing not the Divine sensual delight.*** *Fools they are, who strive in vain. But do lightning, save men from their bitter ignorance, dispel their sorrow and grief, and grant them wisdom, for by wisdom thou dost rule with power and justice. In return for thy blessing we give thee and thy work our everlasting praise. And there is no greater glory for men or for gods than to praise forever* ***Universal Reason."***

**Jupiter de Smyrne, Louvre Museum, circa 250 AD. Sculptor unknown.**
Original restored around 1686.
The Vajra style lightning bolt can be seen clearly in this statue.

## COMMENTARIES

**worshiped under many names** - This phrase reflects the eclectic nature of ancient religions. They did not see a reason to oppose one god against the other, but viewed the different national gods as different titles given to the same forces or principles of nature.

heaven's double-edged thunderbolt of imperishable fire, pulsing its way through every creature that obeys thee - The double-edged thunderbolt is an ancient universal symbol, which can be found as far back as the Hindu Rig Veda, as the *Vajra.*

A fire that is imperishable is not a physical fire. It is life in its deepest sense. To obey Zeus is to obey the laws of Nature; it is to not raise obstacles in the flow of life.

**Universal Reason** – for the Stoics, our intelligence is a reflection of universal intelligence, just as our body is made of elements taken from the material universe. That is, reason is not subjective, but is based on the perception of higher truths.

**but even such discords you know how to weave into a total harmony** - This phrase implies that what seems unjust to the human being, may be just in the larger scale of things. As philosopher Jorge Livraga once said: "What is true for human beings, is a lie for the gods."

**the Law of Reason which blind men cannot understand** - Blindness here indicates the inability to see with the light of intelligence. Everything flows towards harmony, yet we who are blinded by external events, are stuck to a chord of disharmony, unable to see it resolved into greater harmony.

**Instead they suffer loss when they seek happiness in their own fashion, knowing not the Divine sensual delight.** - What does it mean to seek happiness in our own fashion? The oration speaks of the temporary nature of human happiness - the pursuit of riches, power, status, pleasure, etc.

Divine happiness is the happiness that results from finding the divine within us, and by following, with love, the path traced out for us by the Gods.

## CHRYSSYPUS OF SOLI – THE 2nd FOUNDER OF STOICISM

*"If there had been no Chrysippus, there would have been no Stoicism."*
*(Diogenes Laertius)*

Despite being a central figure in the history of Stoicism, not much has been left to us from the hundreds of writings of Chryssypus. He studied with Cleanthes and the Platonists, and organized the Stoic teachings, forming them into a coherent doctrine.

**Chryssipus of Soli, The British Museum.**
**Roman copy of Greek original, 3rd century BC.**
Sculptor unknown.

The best we can do is to present some of his interesting thoughts quoted by Cicero and Epictetus:

*"He who is running a race ought to endeavor and strive to the utmost of his ability to come off victor; but it is utterly wrong for him to trip up his competitor, or to push him aside. So in life it is not unfair for one to seek for himself what may accrue to his benefit; but it is not right to take it from another." (Cicero, De Officiis)*

*"If I knew that it was fated for me to be sick, I would even wish for it; for the foot also, if it had intelligence, would volunteer to get muddy." (Epictetus, Discourses, ii. 6. 10.)*

*"The universe itself is God and the universal outpouring of its soul." (Cicero, De Natura Deorum)*

*"We should infer in the case of a beautiful dwelling-place that it was built for its owners and not for mice; we ought, therefore, in the same way to regard the universe as the dwelling-place of the gods." (Cicero, De Natura Deorum, iii. 10.)*

## MIDDLE STOA: TO ROME

The Athenian Stoic school had in all seven official undisputed scholarchs (heads), the last of whom was Panaetius, who died around 110 BC, and was an important member of the Scipionic circle – a circle of philosophers, poets and writers formed by Scipio Africanus the Younger, an enlightened leader of the Roman Republic. This circle of friends discussed the heritage of Hellenic culture, and probably played an important part in the transmission of Stoicism to Rome.

Less than a century later, Julius Caesar would cross the Rubicon and transform the republic into an empire. Thus, Stoicism and the Roman Empire were close from the start.

Another person influential in making Stoicism popular in Rome was Cicero, a memorable Roman politician. A classical eclectic philosopher, Cicero pursued the understanding of the various Greek schools of philosophy.

In his later life, Cicero's only daughter, Tullia, died after child birth. Like with many others, the experience of grief led Cicero to question what he knew about life, driving him deeper into the study of philosophy. He left the hustle and bustle of Rome, and retired to his villa in Tusculum, where he wrote the *Tusculan Disputations*, in which Cicero discusses with his friend Brutus the teachings of the Greek philosophy schools, including the Stoics, explaining them to the Roman reading public, undoubtedly moved by reflections

regarding his daughter's, and perhaps his own yet unknown, impending death.

The Disputations discuss issues that every human being needs to face at a certain point in life – death, pain, grief, emotions, and above all, the question of a happy life. In agreement with the Stoics, Cicero places virtue on the highest pedestal, pointing out that it is the only thing that brings peace of mind, and therefore happiness.

*"Just as a field, however good the ground, cannot be productive without cultivation, so the soul cannot be productive without teaching. So true it is that the one without the other is ineffective. Now the cultivation of the soul is philosophy; this pulls out vices by the roots and makes souls fit for the reception of seed, and commits to the soul or, as we may say, sows in it seed of a kind to bear the richest fruit." (Cicero, Tusculan Disputations)*

We may ask ourselves why Stoicism, especially its ethical aspects, found such a listening ear in Rome, so much so, as to be almost designated as the "official" philosophy of the Roman empire.

As things are accepted where they are needed, perhaps the Roman way of life, with its strong military tradition and practical approach required the mental and ethical framework to face challenges and to give meaning to everyday actions.

It is also interesting to consider why Stoicism is experiencing a major revival in our times.

It may be that Stoicism is filling a vacuum of moral direction that was previously filled by other channels.

Religion, the sole purpose of which is to provide moral guidelines based on spiritual insights, has become too much of this world for many people, entangled with politics and immorality, as well as with an overly literal and dogmatic interpretation of the sacred scriptures. At the same time, the secular tradition, while very clear about what it does not believe and accept, is much more vague on what it proposes to replace religion with, creating an existential emptiness, avoided through entertainment, consumerism and sensuality. At the same time, modern science, despite making tremendous progress in the understanding of the physical world, has not been able to provide solutions in the realm of ethics. And technology has not made human beings one iota better, as having a smart-phone doesn't make a person any smarter than a person who has a rotary phone or even one who transmits messages with smoke signals.

In times like these, moral philosophy comes to the rescue. People need guidelines, road signs, stepping stones. Stoic philosophy in particular offers all these, and while it may not have all the answers, it opens a window towards more clarity. And clarity, in times of chaos, is a divine boon.

## LATE STOA – EDUCATION TO WISDOM

With the gradual integration of Stoicism into Roman culture, we once again see the dream of Plato reemerging in the annals of history - the dream of a philosophical Aristocracy and the Philosopher-King.

Is there more to leadership than administrating a bureaucracy and achieving certain numbers and statistical marks?

According to the classical view, the power of leadership is found first and foremost in the leader as a model. By the force of example, both morality and immorality "trickle down" from the leaders of a society to its citizens. It is much easier, however, to imitate a negative example than a positive one.

This was the foundation of the Platonic idea of a philosophical Aristocracy (literally, rule of the best), as well as the Confucian ideal of the Junzi (the gentleman). In the heart of democracy as well is the idea that a cultured, informed and educated people will choose the best among themselves to rule. But how to form good leaders? According to Plato and Confucius, it all begins with education.

In Ancient Rome, just like in our days, the type and quality of education children received depended very much on their class and expected duty. Most people studied in voluntary elementary schools to gain basic skills required for workers, soldiers and so on. Social mobility according to inner merits and qualities existed but was rare. The Roman elite employed private tutors (frequently Greek slaves) to gain access to higher studies such as rhetoric, required for law and politics, sciences and poetry. Philosophy was considered the highest discipline, acquired through study in philosophy schools or with philosophy tutors.

An initial attempt to create a philosophical ruler and merge wisdom with leadership, through the education of emperor Nero by Seneca, failed miserably, demonstrating perhaps that it is not enough to transmit philosophical knowledge and example, but that there has to be good "human material" to work with. That is, even the best sculptor with the best tools, will find it hard to sculpt in titanium. Nero did not have the disposition of a philosopher-ruler, but quite the opposite. Seneca's initial influence restrained Nero's negative inclinations, but the longer Nero was in power, the more his true nature revealed itself. This ended tragically, and Seneca was ordered to commit suicide in one of Nero's many purges.

Later attempts, however, were more successful, with the ascent of the Five Good Emperors, a period of around a hundred years, described by the famous historian Gibbon as the period in which the human race was most happy and prosperous. These Five Good Emperors were influenced by Stoicism which by that point had become almost a civil religion in Rome, and the bread and butter of Aristocratic Roman education.

The last of the Five Good Emperors was the famous Marcus Aurelius who was succeeded by his biological son Commodus. In one of the greatest ironies of history, with the narcissistic Commodus, who thought himself to be a reincarnation of Hercules and renamed Rome after himself, a hundred years of ethical leadership came to an end, and a descent began, according to one historian of the times Cassius Dio, "from a kingdom of gold to one of iron and rust."

We have in our possession complete writings of the late Stoa philosophers, as well as biographical and analytical books written about them. Therefore, we are not going to attempt and give a full review of them here, but will simply provide a short introduction to their lives and works.

## SENECA THE YOUNGER (4BC - 65AD)

*"I follow nature; it is common sense not to stray from it but to be molded according to its law and example." (Seneca, A Happy Life [De Vita Beata])*

Seneca was probably the most eloquent exponent of Stoicism and its applications in everyday situations. Marcus Aurelius wrote to himself, Epictetus spoke arrows of truth, but Seneca was a pedagogue of Stoicism; he wrote his books to explain, elucidate, clarify. And while we may argue about his success in applying the teaching he disseminated, we cannot argue the quality of his instructions.

Seneca received his philosophical education through Stoic and Neo-Pythagorean teachers, and quickly became active in the politics of his day.

His was the formidable task of making the first attempt to train a philosopher-emperor in the style of Plato's philosopher-king. Unfortunately, the human material he had to work with did not stand to the task. The object of Seneca's tutoring was Nero Claudius Caesar, who rose to absolute power at the age of 16, after decades of unstable government. Nero, however, revealed himself as unable to apply or even perceive the philosophical ideas of his teacher.

Seneca's understanding and presentation of Stoicism in his books is impeccable. Yet, he had the terrible challenge of trying to live a Stoic life in the midst of corruption and bloodshed. The key dilemma of his life was the question of how can we be good when everything around us is bad? How can we influence without being influenced?

At a certain point, Seneca chose to retire and distance himself from court life, but his karma followed him. At the age of 68 he was implicated in a conspiracy to assassinate Nero and was ordered to commit suicide, which he aspired to comply with, in the Socratic spirit. Four years later Nero himself committed suicide.

## THE LETTERS OF SENECA

Like in the *Meditations* by Marcus Aurelius, the letters of Seneca reveal the honest inner reflections of a Stoic philosopher, who in this case does not speak to himself, but to a young brother on the path, guiding him in the art of facing life's difficulties with the help of Philosophy.

The moral letters to Lucillus were written by Seneca towards the end of his life, and deal with everything from gladiators and slaves to asthma and politics. Seneca masterfully shows how every aspect of life can be given meaning and depth with the help of philosophy, how everything in life can be connected with the thread of wisdom.

*"Happy the man who improves other people not merely when he is in their presence but even when he is in their thoughts!"*

## GAIUS MUSONIUS RUFUS (c.30 – c.101AD)

*"As a noble example of the good life, Musonius would be an outstanding character in any age; against the background of spiritual passivity and moral decay of his own generation, he appears a truly heroic figure". (Lutz)*

*"The study of philosophy is nothing else than to search out by reason what is right and proper and by deeds to put it into practice." (Musonius Rufus)*

Known primarily today as the teacher of Epictetus, in his time and in the centuries following his death Musonius Rufus was considered no less than a Roman Socrates.

We do not know where and from whom Rufus learned Stoic philosophy but in his teachings he already establishes the principles according to which Stoicism will be later known and which were brought into practice by great later Stoics like Epictetus and Marcus Aurelius.

For Rufus ethics took the first place among the Stoic disciplines;

philosophy has to be put into practice and not just remain an intellectual exercise.

As a practical philosopher, he dealt with questions on the very concrete themes that occupied the minds of his disciples, including work, marriage, food, parents, old age, and so on. The philosopher must live in the world, and philosophy should be able to respond the real needs of everyday life.

It was in exile, however, that Rufus proved himself not just as a theoretician but as a real practitioner of the Stoic art of living. Annoyed by his popularity, Nero exiled him to Gyaros, an arid and unpopulated island in the northern Cyclades, the 'Alcatraz' of Roman times, which even the Emperor Tiberius considered too cruel a punishment, "harsh and devoid of human culture". Nevertheless, Rufus was able to transform his exile into an opportunity. He personally uncovered a source of fresh water and began working the soil, together with students who joined him in exile. Groups of students travelled to listen and work with him, and Gyaros became an unlikely centre of philosophy.

In his lectures, Rufus refers to his exile and denies its absolute negativity. He presents farming as an ideal occupation to practice and teach philosophy. He invites the aspiring philosopher once again to look within and remember that the ultimate purpose is to develop one's virtues:
*"Certainly the exile is not prevented from possessing courage and justice simply because he is banished, nor is he denied self-control or any virtue that brings honor and benefit to the man with a good reputation and worthy of praise... If you are good, you will never be harmed or degraded by exile, for your virtues will help you and sustain you. But if you are bad, it is the evil that harms you and not exile, and the misery you feel in exile is the product of evil, not of exile." (from the 9th Discourse)*

# THE STOIC OPPOSITION

*"Nero having butchered so many illustrious men, at last aspired to extirpate virtue itself by murdering Thrasea Paetus and Barea Soranus." (Tacitus)*

It was dangerous to be a Stoic under the rule of Nero.

With his usual insight, Plato writes in *The Republic* that a tyrant will act to clear out the best elements of society, which are the most virtuous and moral of its citizens, and establish his circle of "drones" in power, the worst and most odious elements. Nero, a model tyrant, followed this prediction like a play book.

The first of the three prominent citizens and Stoics to be killed by Nero was Rubellius Plautus, a relative of Nero, who was a senator and a good friend, probably a disciple, of the prominent Stoic Gaius Musonius Rufus. His virtues and high moral standards placed him in the eyes of the people as a contender for the crown, and he was executed while in exile, his estates given to Nero's wife.

His friend Barea Soranus, governor of Asia Minor, was tried in a mock trial for treason, and for practicing magic and astrology with his daughter, against the emperor. Both he and his daughter were ordered to commit suicide. Ironically, the main witness against Soranus was his household philosopher, Egnatius Celer - a clear traitor to the Stoic teachings and an example of one who demonstrates that Stoicism can also be nothing more than lip service. Later on, after Nero's time, he too was put to trial and executed, convicted due to the incriminating testimony of Musonius Rufus.

The last of the Stoic martyrs was Thrasea Paetus, a model of the lost Roman virtues of dignitas and libertas. Thrasea was not willing to participate in a ceremony of adulation to Nero, after the tyrant had executed his own mother. Under the charge of treason he too was ordered to commit suicide.

The Stoic beliefs of these senators and politicians were put to a harsh test by the corruption and evil of the times. And by their choices they exemplified one of the major Stoic teachings. They aimed to be indifferent to the life and death of the body, while valuing the supreme importance of the life and death of the soul.

In this they followed Socrates, who obeyed his *daimon*, the inner voice that guided him in his ethical actions and told him what to avoid and how not to act. When Socrates was put on trial and sentenced to death, he said that his inner *daimon* did not object, which must mean that death is not as terrible as most people think.

## EPICTETUS (55 - 135 AD)

Being owned by another person, is the antithesis of what we imagine as freedom. Yet from this state of slavery, the Stoic philosopher Epictetus evolved the highest ideal of freedom - the freedom from oneself.

Being a slave, Epictetus had to make a choice we all know well, but in much more severe circumstances.

Will I let circumstances dictate my life, or will I be the captain of my soul, finding opportunities for growth, which although unseen, are hidden everywhere, in every minute?

Nelson Mandela and Etti Hillesum are some modern historical examples of the Epictetian spirit of freedom without limits. They demonstrated that a chained person can sometimes be freer than those who chain him.

While Epictetus himself, as far as we know, did not write anything, his teachings were gathered and put into writing by his disciple Arrian, a passionate historian and philosopher.

Using his own lecture notes, Arrian wrote a user-friendly guide to Stoicism called the "Epictetus Manual" (In Greek *Enchiridion Epiktetoi*), a synthesis of his teacher's thoughts in easy-to-digest paragraphs which can be understood and applied by any person. In thinking about future generations and not about his own originality, Arrian made an essential contribution to the history of ideas.

Epictetus taught that the first step to freedom is discernment. Recognize what is in our power, and what is not, and accept what is not in our power. We desire things to be different, we are unwilling to surrender ourselves to life, to the Gods. If we let go of our resistance, we will find freedom.

*With every incident, ask yourself what abilities you have for making a proper use of it. If you see an attractive person, you will find that self-restraint is the ability you have against your desire. If you are in pain, you will find fortitude. If you hear unpleasant language, you will find patience. And thus habituated, the appearances of things will not hurry you away along with them.*

Every situation in life hides a treasure. It conceals a quality which is calling us to bring it forth. Judging the situation from a limited and subjective perspective, we are the ones who close the lid on these opportunities for growth, disguised as obstacles. We judge life by comparing it to our expectations, and to what we like or don't like. But life is not here to be judged or rated, it is to be lived. If you want to know why a certain situation appears in your life, ask yourself: What are you learning from it?

*Remember that you are an actor in a drama, of such a kind as the author pleases to make it. If short, of a short one; if long, of a long one. If it is his pleasure you should act a poor man, a cripple, a governor, or a private person, see that you act it naturally. For this is your business, to act well the character assigned you; to choose it is another's.*

A common saying in theater: There are no small roles, only small actors. The important thing is not what is our role, but how do we play that role. Daniel Day-Lewis plays in one movie the role of a ruthless oil baron, a fashion designer in another, and an American president in a third. What makes him a great actor is that whichever role he plays, he is that, and there are no doubts in the viewer's mind about it. We have been given a role and that role is ours. We need to be the best of who we are. Perhaps we don't have the best cards in the deck, but we can play and have a great game with what we do have. And we always have something to give. In the words of the Bhagavad Gita: It is better to realize your own role (Swadharma) imperfectly than to live a perfect imitation of somebody else's.

*I am no immortal, but a man, a part of the sum of things as an hour is of a day. Like the hour, I must arrive, like the hour, I must pass away.*

Anything that arrives must go. Life is a series of encounters and farewells. If we recognize this we can appreciate our relationships, and at the same time accept they are temporary and not attach to them in an unhealthy way.

**The Double Herm of Socrates and Seneca, Pergamon Museum, Berlin. 3rd century AD.**
Unknown Sculptor.
Seneca as a martyr of philosophy, similar to Socrates.

The final entry of the Enchiridion, or Handbook, begins: "Upon all occasions we ought to have these maxims ready at hand."

*Conduct me, Zeus, and thou, O Destiny,*
*Wherever thy decree has fixed my lot.*
*I follow willingly; and, did I not,*
*Wicked and wretched would I follow still.*
(Diogenes Laertius quoting Cleanthes;
quoted also by Seneca, Epistle 107)

*Whoe'er yields properly to Fate is deemed*
*Wise among men, and knows the laws of Heaven.*
(Euripides, Fragments 965)

*O Crito, if it thus pleases the gods, thus let it be.*
(Plato, Crito)

*Anytus and Meletus may indeed kill me, but they cannot harm me.*
(Plato, Apology)

## MARCUS AURELIUS (121 – 180 AD)
The Philosopher Emperor

Marcus Aurelius is without doubt one of the most impressive figures of western history. A philosopher and emperor (in that order), he proved that philosophy doesn't have to be disconnected from reality. Stoicism helped Marcus to confront, with dignity and mindfulness, the terrible difficulties of being a ruler of a vast empire.

We find many occurrences where good-willed and idealistic people lose their moral compass on gaining positions of power, and it is common knowledge that absolute power corrupts absolutely. Great historical figures, however, such as Abraham Lincoln, Charles de Gaulle and Nelson Mandela, as well as Marcus Aurelius himself - who all had great power, yet held onto a clear ethical axis - put to doubt this affirmation.

Perhaps it is truer that power reveals rather than corrupts. Those who are "untouchable", like Elliot Ness in the famous movie, remain untouchable.

As Plato already discussed, incorruptibility is an altitude and aptitude of the soul which can be trained. It prepares and shields us from putting material temptations over the greater good. It can be left to chance, or play a part in a philosophical education to leadership.

An emperor of Rome makes decisions that affect the lives and deaths of many every day, he participates in bloody battles, and constantly appoints and fires leaders and officials. Just 70 years earlier Domitian used the emperor's powers to make himself sole Augustus of the Roman Empire and effectively dispense with the senate as a political power in the state. And let us not forget Nero, who we already mentioned, and who ordered the execution of his own mother, and his teacher and adviser Seneca.

Marcus Aurelius, however, took his duty as an emperor, with all its hardships, as a sacred duty. Throughout his career he had to face multiple invasions, economic crises and a disastrous plague which decimated about 5 million people across Europe.

He was a disciple who held his teachers in such high esteem

**Gold Coin portraying Marcus Aurelius, 167/168 AD, Art Institute of Chicago**
Marcus Aurelius is shown wielding his distinctive philosopher's beard.

that he kept gold portraits of them in his private shrine and honored their tombs with personal visits, offering flowers and sacrifices in their memory. He greeted his teacher, Junius Rusticus, with a kiss, an honor upon among the highest members of the senate.

His *Meditations*, which he mostly wrote while on military campaigns, is a testimony to his lofty ideals, and to the fact that like every philosopher, he was aware of his imperfections, but constantly strove to unite himself with the image of the sage, to become one with the ideal he envisioned.

The quality of *Meditations* cannot be overstated. It is a glimpse into the mind of a great emperor and philosopher, and it is a glimmer of hope, because it proves that sometimes, for reasons unknown to us, history generously provides us with leaders who are sincerely good and of high consciousness.

*"Let it make no difference to thee whether thou art cold or warm, if thou art doing thy duty; and whether thou art drowsy or satisfied with sleep; and whether ill-spoken of or praised; and whether dying or doing something else. For it is one of the acts of life, this act by which we die: it is sufficient then in this act also to do well what we have in hand." (Marcus Aurelius, Meditations, Book 6)*

# PART III

# STOICISM TODAY

As a general rule of thumb, the best way to get acquainted with the teachings of the Stoics is through their own writings, which are easily accessible, coherent, and direct. There is no need for any preparation in order to approach them.

Of course, we must take into account that the majority of what has remained comes from the period of the Late Stoa, from the likes of Seneca, Epictetus (through Arrian) and Marcus Aurelius.

The following chapter will include a few reflections on the teachings of the Stoics and their application in 21st century life, and does not aim to provide a complete review of their teachings.

## WHAT CAN WE CHANGE?

*"Of things some are in our power, and others are not." (Epictetus)*

The above statement may seem obvious and clear to our intellect, but the real problem in Stoicism, and in the practice of philosophy in general, does not lie in understanding the teachings, **but in minimizing the gap between what we understand, and how we act.**

What is beyond our control?
We can't control the weather and the stars.
We can't control the circumstances of our birth: what family we were born into, our ethnicity and nationality, our biological heritage.
We can't control the fact that we will die, nor the circumstances of our death.
We can't control the actions, thoughts and emotions of others.
We can't control the actions taken by us or others in the past, nor the consequences of these actions.

It is relatively easy to understand these things, but it is much more difficult to accept their ramifications and to live accordingly, especially when we understand them only with our intellect, and not with our whole being.

To accept that some things are not in our power, means to let go of the illusion of control. This doesn't mean that we cannot try and affect or change things, but that we develop a healthy detachment from the results of our actions, truly realizing that the facts of life are not affected by our opinions of them.

To recognize what we can change, and what we can't, requires discernment.

To see reality as it is and to accept it, requires strength and dignity. And to build this inner resilience is within our power.

## CAN WE BE HAPPY?

The pursuit of happiness is one of the pillars of modern society and has always been of interest to humanity in general. Both Plato and Aristotle saw happiness as the only thing human beings desire for its own sake. In a later period, Thomas Jefferson, inspired by the philosophers of the Enlightenment, defined the pursuit of happiness as one of the three inherent and inalienable rights of the US constitution, together with life and liberty.

It is a natural wish, to be happy.

Seneca wrote, however, that while we all wish to be happy, if we are to search for happiness in the wrong direction, then naturally, the more we will pursue happiness the farther away we will get from it.

Clearly, it is important to reflect then on the meaning of happiness and to make sure our choices lead towards it. Otherwise our pursuit of happiness itself may lead us exactly to unhappiness.

If we retrace the etymological origin of the word happiness, we find it comes from the old Norse *hap*, which means fortune or luck, as in haphazard. This equates happiness with being fortunate, which is a passive condition, and completely dependent on external circumstances.

Originally, the word happiness was an unfortunate translation of the Greek word *eudaimonia* which was used by the Greek philosophers to denote the purpose of life, and the aspired for inner state of the practice of philosophy.

*Eudaimonia* can be related to the inner *daimon*, the inner voice Socrates listened to when making ethical decisions in life. It is the voice of conscience, the Tibetan voice of the silence. Aristotle defined *Eudaimonia* as an activity guided by virtue.

Happiness as *Eudaimonia* is the serenity that accompanies a purposeful and pure-hearted way of life. It is going to bed at peace with yourself, knowing that you gave everything to life.

We can therefore speak of two different perceptions of happiness.

The first equates happiness with luck, fortune, and a somewhat vague feeling of well-being. The second, *Eudaimonia*, equates happiness with living well.

Happiness, in the first sense, is completely dependent on circumstances, and is pursued by chasing external rewards.

*Eudaimonia* depends on us and springs from our inner world when we act in accordance with our nature.

## YOU CAN'T ALWAYS GET WHAT YOU WANT?

*"Accept the things to which fate binds you, and love the people with whom fate brings you together, but do so with all your*

*heart." (Marcus Aurelius)*

Nobody likes to be disappointed. Disappointment, however, is a part of life. But must it be?

When we desire something and we don't get it, we are disappointed. When we are averse to something and it shows up in our life, we are disappointed. One way to avoid disappointments then is to get everything we desire or think we desire, and to avoid everything we are averse to.

But Epictetus's first dictum (and common sense) tells us that not everything is in our power. Therefore it seems impossible to get everything we desire and avoid everything we don't like. In truth, this is also undesirable. As philosophers and human beings, we seek to grow, and this approach is nothing less than trying at all costs to remain in our comfort zone.

Nevertheless, there's still a way to get everything we desire and to avoid disappointments. How? Epictetus tells us that we must train *"the domain of desires and aversions, so that we may not find ourselves frustrated in our desires, and may not encounter that which we are seeking to avoid."*

We can do this by changing what we desire and what we are averse to. If we can desire and be averse to things that are in our control, then we can avoid disappointment.

What is in our control?
Whether we act ethically or not, in response to life's responsibilities and provocations, is the only truly important thing in the eyes of the Stoics and the only thing that is completely in our power. Therefore, if we desire to act well, and are averse to not acting well, then being disappointed will depend solely on ourselves.

Some things may be preferable to others, for example health

over illness, wealth over poverty. But as these things are not completely in our control, if we desire them strongly, eventually we are going to be disappointed.

Therefore, at the end of the day, to desire the morally good, and to avoid the morally evil, is the most rational approach, as these are the only things which completely depend on us and not on circumstances. At every crossroad in life, we are the owners of our actions.

Contentment then is not a result of getting what you want. But of truly doing the best you can.

In the domain of desires and aversions, Epictetus also tells us to "follow the Gods", in other words, to accept those things which are beyond our control, and are consequences of the laws of nature, or the will of universal nature.

If we do not recognize the laws of nature, and learn to accept them, we will be disappointed. Simply because the laws of nature do not change to adapt to our so-called important desires, just as an elephant does not move out of its way for an ant. We are the ones who need to adapt.

## WHO ARE THE GODS?

Human beings have always tried to understand the events taking place around them, and especially those they cannot control.

There is an ancient and pervasive intuition among all the peoples of mankind of an existence of some intelligence or power, beyond the limits of our understanding. This intuition has been called by many names.

Among the ancient Greeks and Romans, it was called Theoi, or the Gods. The gods appear frequently in the writings of the Stoics, but not in the sense of a supernatural intervention in the course of nature. On the contrary, the gods are higher aspects of nature, which are reflected in the world through its laws and mysteries. They are mysteries not because they cannot be known, but because we are ignorant of their true nature.

A dolphin, swimming leisurely on the waves of his great oceanic world, may choke on a plastic bag, or sense the changing temperatures of the waters. However, it cannot even slightly perceive the ideas of pollution, recycling, or climate change, yet it feels their effects each and every day. The human ability of abstract thought is so far removed from the dolphin that it almost belongs to a different dimension. For the animals that live around us, we are like gods (or perhaps demons).

The Gods are representatives of the Imagination. Today, we frequently use the word imagination to connote something that is unreal - a fantasy, a figment of our imagination: "it's just your imagination". Imagination, however, in contrast to fantasy, is precisely to see beyond the visible.

For example, when I make plans to meet someone in a week, I use my imagination to project myself towards a future time and place, which does not exist as yet.

And when this meeting takes place, this imaginary projection will have become materialized. This ability to see into the nonexistent, into the unknown, is a uniquely human power.

There are ways to penetrate the mysteries of nature and come closer to the gods. Suffice it to say, that the ancient philosophers believed it is not the gods who will come down to us, but that it is us who must come closer to them, by becoming more like them.

We tend to ignore or disregard those things which do not sit well within our world-view. The appearance of gods in the Stoic doctrine can be foreign to both modern religious and scientific thinkers. This is because we have been taught to consider the gods as a subject for a bed time story or a Disney movie, and not a subject for a serious inquisitive mind. And yet, the last thing we could say about the Stoic philosophers was that they were gullible fools who took bedtime stories seriously.

Although it is hard to admit it, we still don't know a lot about the universe, nature, life and even ourselves. Science has made undeniable progress in the understanding and application of the mechanisms of physical nature. Yet, in regards to the Why of things, of the deeper reasons, of the meaning of life, we are still as (or more) blind as Neanderthal man. We have our opinions, but nothing more.

When we speak of the sacred dimension of life, which unfortunately has been sacrificed together with the excesses of institutionalized religion, we speak of that Mystery, of the Other, that which can only be seen with the heart, in the words of the Little Prince. It does not belong to any religion.

The Stoics were deeply in touch with that unknown element. They acknowledged the universal entities which can only be perceived by the use of the imagination.

They invite us to live with the Sacred, so our lives won't be empty and superficial. They invite us to become vertical human beings, each one a bridge between the invisible and the visible.

As Epictetus writes beautifully: *"If I were a nightingale, I would perform the work of a nightingale, and if I were a swan, that of a swan. But as it is, I am a rational being, and I must sing the praise of God. This is my work, and I accomplish it, and I will never abandon my post for as long as it is granted to me to remain in it; and I invite all of you to join me in this same song." (Discourses 1.16.20-21)*

## CAN WE TRUST OUR FEELINGS?

Human beings are often said to be rational creatures, but in reality we are very much emotional creatures as well. More often than not, history is a showcase of tragic actions taken by human beings overcome by their passions. And apart from these grand dramas, everyday life is full of instances where the right thing is sacrificed for the sake of an urge, the ego, the instinct.

In great theatrical tragedies, such as Shakespearean *King Lear* or *Romeo and Juliet*, the passionate actions taken by the protagonists lead to an unfortunate chain of events of betrayal and death.

This is the fate of characters in great dramas, but how many times the small dramas of our everyday lives have developed in negative ways because of our lack of control? How many times have our passionate actions led us to a deep, dark hole?

In order to develop the necessary mastery over our emotions, the Stoics recommended we should observe and understand them first, deconstruct them by recognizing their true nature. In their writings we find a startling analysis, almost a system, of the various emotions and their causes.

At the center of their psychological teachings we find the concept of *pathes*, unhealthy passions, agitations of the soul that are contrary to reason or nature. Those are the emotions which lead us to act against our nature, and against our best interest. It is interesting that the Greeks used the same word *pathos* (πἄθος) to indicate both passion, and suffering. Today we use this Greek root in the words Pathology (the study of suffering), and Apathy (the lack of passion).

The Stoics, beginning with Zeno and Hecato, divide the passions into four groups[1]:

---

1. English definitions are based on the translation of Cicero's *Tusculan Disputations* by J. E. King.

*Epithumia* – Craving or strong desire
A desire to possess something that holds an ***apparent*** gain for us. Anger, for example is an expression of craving, defined as the desire for punishing the person thought to have inflicted an undeserved injury.

*Phobos* – Fear
A belief of threatening evil which ***seems*** unbearable to its subject. Some examples are fear of disgrace and the fear of impending work.

*Hêdonê* – Pleasure
Newly formed ***belief*** of present good, and the subject thinks it right to feel enraptured. Malice is one type of such pleasure, which is the enjoyment of another's ills.

*Lupê* – Sorrow (form of suffering)
A newly formed ***belief*** of present evil, the subject of which thinks it right to feel depression and shrinking of soul. Envy, a distress caused by another person's prosperity, is a form of irrational sorrow.

As can be seen, the passions are based on *appearances*, that is, of our interpretation of reality. They result from **false value judgments.**

Objective reality makes an impression *(phantasia)* on our souls. This impression feeds the passion and causes us to react.

The philosopher aims to reflect *(dianoia)* on the true nature of these impressions, and guided by the inner *hegemonikon*, our ruling part, to act according to true value judgments. The philosopher is vigilant, observes within, and is not led by impressions. He chooses to act according to reason.

For example, we may feel craving for a certain object, thinking it will be good for us. Yet we all know that many times we crave for things that are clearly not good for us, i.e. junk food or other addictions. In that sense, we are acting against our best interest, that is, we are acting irrationally. We are prioritizing our short-term self at the expense of our long-term self.

Isn't that the definition of **ignorance**, mentioned so often by the Buddhists and the Greek philosophers as the greatest evil? That is, the false perception that what is good is bad and vice versa? The poison is seen as a blessing, and the blessing as poison.

We cannot trust our feelings so long as they are not purified by the light of reason. The aim is to release ourselves from the effect of ignorance-based passions, and to nurture the positive sentiments of the sage – joy, caution and wishing.

THE SENTIMENTS OF THE SAGE

The sage is not portrayed as a cold, apathetic person. By reflecting on the good and the bad, and on the true nature of things, the sage develops natural, rational sentiments – *hai eupatheiai*, literally, the good passions. These are: Wish, Caution and Joy.

Joy [*chara*], the counterpart of pleasure - rational elation.
Caution [*eulabeia*], the counterpart of fear - rational avoidance.
Wishing [*boulesis*], the counterpart of craving - rational appetite.

Joy [*chara*]

If pleasure is caused by an irrational and ignorant perception, rational elation is brought forth by the enjoyment of that which is proper to the human being. This is the joy of contemplating the ideas, of seeing the beauty of nature, of bathing in the light of reason and wisdom.

While we continue to seek pleasures, we lose sight of the beauty all around us. What can we really pursue that is more beautiful than the blue skies? Richer than the human being? Deeper and more interesting than our own selves? As Marcus Aurelius wrote: "Very little is needed to make a happy life, it is all within yourself".

Caution (*eulabeia*)

Plato defined courage as recognizing what we should be afraid of, and what we shouldn't be afraid of. Ideally the philosopher's rational outlook should allow him to avoid all fear, because there's nothing to be afraid of. In the words of Marcus Aurelius: "*What can happen to the Human Being, which is not proper to the Human Being?*"

If the philosopher should avoid all fear, then where does caution come into the picture?

There is a certain logic to avoid unnecessary dangers and hindrances, but we do have to be cautious in order to avoid the dangers of the soul.

Socrates said that a man should have more fear of causing injustice than to be treated unjustly. The health and purity of the soul are as important, if not more, as that of the body.

The philosopher should use utmost caution to avoid putting his soul at risk, that is, to let his soul sink into the abyss of immorality and impurity. It is a subtle form of caution, but the most rational, as it is occupied with taking care of that which is constant, rational and natural. Having caution in regards to the physical survival of the body, which is temporary in any case, is only second to the spiritual survival of the soul.

This means to know ourselves, to recognize those things, whether external or internal, that drag us down, pollute our soul, make us lose our center, and to avoid these things as much as possible. The stronger we are inside, the more resistant we can be to negative external influences. But we also need to have the humility to know which things are beyond our mastery of ourselves, and are better to avoid completely.

Wishing (*boulesis*)
The popular saying "be careful what you wish for" refers to irrational craving - that which we wish for may not always be good for us or others.

However, while the philosopher should avoid irrational craving, this shouldn't be replaced with apathetic, idle, and purposeless living.

Wishing or *Boulesis* is a rational appetite, it is the pursuit of the things that are truly good, for you and for everybody: the virtues, the excellent completion of your duties, the wish to improve the lives of those around you and those for whom you are responsible.

The meditations of Marcus Aurelius and the books of Seneca are full of these everyday wishes, which are a constant motivation for improvement and realization.

And this leads us to another question: Should one's good life come at the expense of another's?

In a highly competitive society like ours, one's success means another's failure. If I get a job, another hundred lose it. In a competitive "Ayn Randish" society there are winners and there are losers. This is the law of the jungle. It is interesting, however, that the word compete originates in the Latin *competere*, which means to strive together.

Will humanity ever establish a society in which one's victory does not mean another's defeat? In which one's strength does not mean another's weakness? In which one's good life does not mean another's miserable one?

So far, we haven't been able to achieve that. Maybe we've been wishing for the wrong things?

In the spirit of the Stoics, we can only answer that everything is natural. And as in nature, everything will balance out eventually.

## APPENDIX

There are several versions of the sub-divisions of the passions, as this is more subjective and can be interpreted in different ways. Precise categorization of the various emotions can be like deciding if a certain color is mauve or magenta (both shades of purple), it is much less clear cut than the more discernible difference between blue and red for example.

In the following table the definitions of both Diogenes Laertius [*The Eminent Lives of Philosophers, Tran: R. D. Hicks*], and Cicero [*The Tusculan Disputations, Tran: J.E. King*] are used.

| **Craving or Desire** | **Real essence** | **Comments** |
|---|---|---|
| Greed | insatiable lust for money, distinctions, etc. | |
| Longing | Unrequited love or a desire for an unattainable object | |
| Contentiousness | | |
| Anger | Desire for punishing the person thought to have inflicted an undeserved injury | |
| Love (eros) | An effort to win affection due to the visible presence of beauty. | This is separate from the more subtle aspects of eros, which relate to higher levels of attraction than the body. |
| Wrath | anger of greater bitterness conceived in the innermost heart and soul | |
| Resentment | Anger at an early stage. | |
| Hatred | A growing and lasting desire or craving that it should go ill with somebody. | |

| Fear | Real essence | Comments |
|---|---|---|
| Terror | Fright – Paralyzing Fear | |
| Shame | Fear of disgrace | |
| Agony | Fear resulting from suspense | |
| Sluggishness | Fear of impending work | |
| Consternation | Fear due to some unusual occurrence | |

| Pleasure | Real essence | Comments |
|---|---|---|
| Malice | Pleasure at another's ills. | |
| Rapture | Pleasure which charms the ear. | |
| Delight | The enjoyment of weakness, of vice. | |

| Sorrow | Real essence | Comments |
|---|---|---|
| Envy | Distress caused by another person's prosperity, although it does not do any harm to oneself. | |
| Jealousy | Distress caused by another's possession of what one wants. | |
| Pity | Distress felt at another's seemingly undeserved suffering. | |
| Rivalry | Distress felt at another's possession of a thing one has. | |
| Vexation | Distress that weights us down. | |
| Trouble, grief, lamenting, etc. | Various forms of lasting and painful distress. | |
| Distraction | Irrational grief, hindering us from viewing the situation as whole. | |

## WHAT DOES IT MEAN TO BE RATIONAL?

Rationality is a central element in the Stoic doctrine, but it is interpreted in a slightly different manner than today. Today, to be rational means to be logical, calculating, and to base our assumptions and conclusions only on what we can see, feel or hear, that is, on our senses.

This type of rationality tends to analyze, that is, it takes things apart, but also prevents us from seeing the unity beyond the parts. It is like seeing a group of islands, not realizing that underneath the water, they are all part of the same land mass. By seeing only the parts, we are misled to believe that the world is irrational, disordered and unjust. It's like hearing only a few parts of a musical piece, or watching sporadic episodes of a TV show. We don't see the big picture.

This leads to a utilitarian "cold" rationality that doesn't take into account the human element or mother nature. It is the root of "RealPolitik" which considers only practical considerations and sees ethics as "unrealistic" and "not pragmatic". That is when the survival of the form and the body becomes the highest priority, and the why of things is lost. But if we care about the survival of the spirit and its ideals then the most realistic and pragmatic thing is in fact to act ethically. Otherwise, we are protecting the flower, and allowing the root to die.

According to the Stoics, reason is *Logos*, the intelligence of the cosmos, it is the reflection of the intelligence of nature within us. To be reasonable then is to act in accordance with Nature.

But Nature is a mystery that invites us to unravel its secrets. It is not just a physical world in the grossest sense. It is a soul, just like us. And to penetrate its soul we need subtler tools than our senses, or the rationality that is based on the senses. We are part of the living universe and we need to go within to find its truths.

It is to see the parts, but also to see that they are parts of a whole. It is to intuit that whole, even if we can't truly conceive it in its totality.

## POLITICALLY CORRECT STOICISM?

*"How much time he gains who does not look to see what his neighbor says or does or thinks, but only at what he does himself, to make it just and holy." (Marcus Aurelius, Meditations, IV, 18)*

Whatever may and will be said about the excesses of political correctness, its original purpose was to provide a moral framework, or guidelines, to encourage an aspect of what the Buddhists refer to as the right speech, that is, not to offend others by speaking without tact or consideration for another's feelings. This is a noble effort originating from the wish to respect others. The fact that we need it is more a reflection of our times than anything else.

But as with everything else we humans do, things tend to go to the extremes. And when political correctness begins to become censorship of ideas, of criticism, of objective observations, then we end up shooting ourselves in the foot.

But at this point, we would like to discuss a different aspect of political correctness, which is the other shoe, that is, the inclination to be offended by harsh or ugly words, or by criticism, whether they are justified or not.

Against the tendency to be offended, the Stoics offer a doctrine of resilience, based on a rational analysis of the situation, and the discernment of false motives and value judgments.

What actually happens when we are offended? If someone would tell us that spiders are ugly, we would most likely not be offended as we don't overly identify ourselves as spiders (unless we're

Spiderman). However, if we were spiders, we would probably find these words offensive and untrue.

Now, the fact that we only take offense if the words refer to us, means that the words in themselves may be ugly, but not necessarily offensive. It is us who are offended.

However, we take these words from that person's mouth and bring them into our hearts, instead of just leaving them where they are. A person is shooting arrows at us, and instead of using our ever present mental energy shield, we are throwing ourselves at the arrows.

Why do we do this?
There is no simple answer, but several reasons come to mind.

- We feel that if we don't react it will somehow make the said things true.
- As the words refer to a certain aspect of our identity, it hurts our ego that someone doesn't love us.
- We think it may be true. And seeing our faults always deters us.
- Offense is the best defense. We use our "sensitivity" in order to gain power.

What is the reality of things?
A person said some things. They are based on that person's thoughts and opinions, and they are his or hers. We may consider them with our reason, to analyze their truthfulness, but they have power only if we grant them power.

This doesn't mean we should not correct another person when necessary and possible, or that we should justify our insensitivity. But developing a healthy "armor" will make us more resilient, and allow us to act according to the reality of things, and not according to our passions and irrational reactions.

*"Remember that it is we who torment, we who make difficulties*

*for ourselves — that is, our opinions do. What, for instance, does it mean to be insulted? Stand by a rock and insult it, and what have you accomplished? If someone responds to insult like a rock, what has the abuser gained with his invective?" (Epictetus, Discourses I, 25.28-29)*

## TO ACCEPT FATE WITH LOVE

*"Lead me, Zeus, and you too, Destiny,*
*To wherever your decrees have assigned me.*
*I follow readily, but if I choose not,*
*Wretched though I am, I must follow still." (Cleanthes)*

*"Fate guides the willing, but drags the unwilling." (Seneca)*

The question of suffering has occupied philosophers since the dawn of history, reaching an apex with Siddhartha Gautama, the "Buddha" in the East, who claimed to have found the antidote for suffering.

The thing is that no matter how rich, beautiful, talented or successful we are, all of us experience suffering at certain points in our lives. This is one of the things we all share as human beings.

Suffering is very much linked to our expectations from life. A person who suffers because of a bad day at work, usually does not think "at least I have work" or "at least I'm not a poor hungry beggar somewhere..."

Thus, while we may jokingly refer to some things as "first world problems", they are real in the sense of the suffering they create. That is because we compare our present situation with what we expect and want from life. Suffering is relative, but we all experience it.

When we suffer, our natural tendency is to find someone or

something to blame for our sufferings. If it is possible we will seek someone to blame, any person who may or may not have some involvement in the situation. If there is no person available, we will blame life, god, the stars, the universe. Sometimes, we recognize that we ourselves are responsible for our suffering, but even then this recognition becomes self-chastisement, we we beat ourselves up, adding pain to suffering.

The Stoic solution to suffering is rooted in the concepts of acceptance and change. According to them the world is governed by certain forces that are not in our control. These mysterious forces, which they sometimes called "gods", are guiding the universe and its inhabitants towards an unknown (at least for us) direction. Our free choice is found in recognizing the guidance of these gods and following it, or at least not resisting it. When we resist it, we suffer.

There are certain aspects of our lives we can influence, change, improve, but where we are most free, is within. We decide how we will react to the dictations of fate.

If we deeply observe our lives, we will notice that while we have influence over certain areas, life sometimes guides us, forcibly if necessary, towards certain ends, and although we tell ourselves it was our doing, looking back we can see clearly that we didn't really have any choice, that sometimes life takes us on a ride and all we can do is just sit back and enjoy the view…

The solution to suffering therefore lies in acceptance. Accepting the things we cannot change.

One of our biggest mistakes is that we constantly try to change others. We focus on their faults instead of focusing on ours. But the simple truth is that we can't change another person. We can inspire another person to change, we can show the way, but the only person we can truly change is ourself.

So, there is no point in obsessing about other peoples' behaviors. What we need to think about is a useful and productive way to act. Every human being has the freedom to act as his conscience dictates and we have the freedom to choose the way we react.

Another essential ethical aspect is to own our decisions.

Nelson Mandela followed what he believed to be the right path to end Apartheid, and eventually he ended up in jail for more than 20 years. He could have chosen not to do anything and be free.

Martin Luther King Jr. knew he may get killed if he continued on his path of redemptive leadership, but in a very stoic way he also knew that he must do the right thing and accept the results, whatever they were.

When Socrates was ordered by the tyrants of Athens to act against his conscience, he refused. In his words, he feared committing injustice more than his own death.

Our responsibility is to do the right thing, and to accept the results as they are. What is certain is that we cannot do the wrong thing in order to get better reactions or results.

## THE MIND – THE PARENT WHO JUST CAN'T SAY NO

*"Nature is enough for everything she asks of us. Luxury has turned her back on nature (… ) pressing man's intelligence into the development of vices. First she began to hanker after things that were inessential, and then after things that were harmful, and finally she handed the mind over to the body and commanded it to be the out and out slave of the body's whim and pleasure." (Seneca, Letter 90)*

Imagine a parent and a child. The child, like every child, continuously asks for things it wants. "I want candy, I want to play, I want to watch TV, I don't want medicine, I don't want to go to school, etc..."

How should a parent respond to these wants? Will he or she give the child everything it wants, unconditionally? Or would parenthood entail a thought process, an inner and outer deliberation, to determine which of these needs are essential and helpful, and which are inessential or worse, harmful?

We too have inside us a parent and a child. A mind and a body.

Our body also has its wants and needs. It needs food and rest, it wants comfort and enjoyment, it wants to avoid pain, to procreate and to survive.

These are legitimate needs, but should they be realized, unconditionally, at all costs? Should they lead us in our lives? Are we our bodies?

Usually, our mind is like the parent who can't say no. It becomes, as Seneca says, the out-and-out slave of the body, constantly occupied in getting those things that the body wants, either directly or indirectly.

But when the mind is left to itself, detached from the body's desires, what is it then?

Then the mind can become an objective observer, that can give the body what it needs, which is not necessarily what it wants.

The parent-child analogy is not perfect, because the body will never grow up to become the mind. But when the relationship between the body and the mind matures, the body can become something important, which is really what it should be, as a messenger, an obedient servant of the mind, a means for the mind to realize its highest ideals.

## CAN WE BE FREE?

Who has a better life? The person who is happy and serene, despite being heavily constrained by circumstances, or the person who has all the resources to do practically anything he wants, but is neither happy nor serene?

This question demonstrates the ideal of freedom as presented by the Stoics.

We tend to think of the freedom to do as the highest form of freedom. Let us say I want to start a business, build a house, establish a career, etc. I will consider everything that blocks me from doing those things as obstacles to my freedom. For the Stoics these things were important, but more important was the freedom to be.

Our external freedom will always be limited by external circumstances, for several reasons. Our freedom cannot come at the expense of another's. We are constrained by the laws of nature, and although we would like to imagine a free society, we are also limited by the constraints of our society, whether just or unjust. We are also limited by the circumstances of our birth, with regards to nationality, finance, education, etc. We can be creative and find ways to extend the scope of our freedom, but there will always be a limit.

The equation is simple. A person who is free is happy, serene and good.

Anything that prevents us from being happy, serene and good, is a chain that enslaves us, regardless of whether it is external or internal. As we cannot control external circumstances all the time, what prevents us from being happy, serene and good is often internal, and is born from our reaction to external circumstances. In that sense, we enslave ourselves.

FREEDOM OR MANIPULATION?

We like to believe that we live in a free world, and yet all of us - with some minor variations - wear the same clothes, eat the same food at the same chain restaurants, share the same habits, use the same technologies...

Either we all have considered all the other options and chosen these as the best, or we are not as free as we think we are.

The marketing and advertisement industry is based, in large part, on the manipulation of desires. Many millions of dollars are spent each year to study how to manipulate human weaknesses.

We are slaves to our desires, and this weakness is used to persuade us to get things we don't need and even harmful to us and to our environment. This weakness is also used to divert us towards one direction or another on the political map.

Images of juicy burgers or fluffy cakes are used to create cravings for foods that are disharmonious, not to say poisonous for our bodies, our sexual desires are yoked to cars and TV shows, and our desire to be loved and appreciated is used to sell us everything from clothing to electronics. But the most powerful manipulation is carried out on our desires for certain things not to happen, or in other words, our fears.

**If we cannot control our desires, we can be easily manipulated.** And the irony is, that this inclination to be manipulated is presented as the image of freedom – the freedom to do whatever I want.

The freedom to do whatever I want, however, curiously coincides with the interests of commerce and the media.

Socrates said that if we put someone in chains, and then let him go, he will feel that sensation we usually call happiness. So the best way to make you feel happy, is to put chains on you and then let you go. Creating the disease and selling the cure.

A desire, however, is never satisfied. It is just quenched temporarily. Thus, we become addicted to the fulfillment of every desire we have, becoming even more enslaved to these temporary alleviators.

In this sense the Stoics have something to tell us about smart consumerism, which in short means - just buy what you need. This is not so easy to do when you grow up in a society of free market capitalism.

Surrounded by endless stimulations, it is very hard to avoid the variety of poisons offered by our modern world, but we can aspire to choose our poison consciously, gradually developing control over ourselves and resistance to external manipulation. This does not result in a life without joy. It means that we must seek out forms of joy that are not injurious, as well as to rediscover the joy in simple things.

*"Events are always closely connected with those which they follow; and all are fitted together harmoniously". (Marcus Aurelius, IV, 45)*

## HOW CAN WE LIVE FULLY?

Sometimes we feel we don't have enough time to accomplish everything we want to. In his essay "On the Brevity of Life" *(De Brevitate Vitae)*, Seneca deals us an important message: it is not that life is short, it is that we don't really use what we have.

The fact that Seneca wrote this essay for Roman readers, shows us that the attempt to use time efficiently, and to avoid wasting time, was something that occupied the minds of ancient people as much as it occupies ours.

It seems, however, that our society has perfected the "art" of wasting time. We have developed hi-end means of distraction, ways to intercept usefulness, to make time bland and meaningless. Moments of sensual stimulation, soon to be forgotten, hijack the qualities of our mind.

Not only do we waste our time, we actually "kill time".

The irony is that if someone dares to put their hands on our property or money we will fight to death for it. And yet we give our time, our most precious resource, to anyone who offers us a slight chance of entertainment.

In keeping with the Stoic teachings, Seneca tells us that our desires enslave us. Our addictions, big and small, pull us towards distraction and waste. Time then becomes like an empty jar, devoid of the substance of life.

What we need is more quality time. Quality time is not just a special time spent with our families or friends. Why not make every second of our lives quality time? Was the time given to us meant to be used only on special occasions? What about quality time with ourselves? With nature?

Quality time is not the same as quantity time. Spending more time on something doesn't necessarily endow it with more quality. The quality time we spend with another person is not measured by the number of words we say. The productivity of our work is not measured by the number of hours we spend in the office.

There are many ways we can put more quality in our time.

- Working efficiently, being useful to our society.
- Having a profound conversation, where we make some progress in understanding each other or the world we live in.
- A meeting with ourselves, just the two of I, reflecting on life and destiny.

- Teaching others, to share our experience, to help other people see things more clearly and suffer less. What can be more productive?

We can choose how to use our time. Don't let anybody take your time from you, it's your most precious resource.

*"Life, if you know how to use it, is long." (Seneca)*

---

# FINAL THOUGHTS

# STOIC PHILOSOPHY FOR OUR TIMES

The pursuit of wisdom and the good life runs like a thread throughout the history of humanity. Among the many groups and individuals who have attempted to propagate a natural philosophy of living, the Stoics stand out both for their persistence and perseverance as a philosophy school, and for their influence on the history of humanity.

It is clear at this point that humanity is going through a crisis of global proportions. And although the symptoms of this crisis are expressed in the environmental, political and economical spheres, the roots of this crisis may be much deeper.

In reality, this is a moral, philosophical and spiritual crisis.

Moral, because we have lost the sense of good and bad. We have rejected and abandoned the traditional beacons which instructed us in the world of morality, but we have not formed any viable alternatives.

Philosophical, because we have lost the sense of what is true and what is false, and above all the inner tools of discernment and reflection that allow us to discern between the two.

Spiritual, because we have lost the sense of the real and the unreal.

We have enthroned the temporary and the fleeting, the material and the coarse, and neglected the eternal spiritual values that have inspired humanity through the ages.

It seems humanity has lost its way. We are like a ship sailing without a compass, without a North Star to guide us. In times like these, philosophy as a way of life, presents a universal, non-denominational and eclectic approach to regain our lost values and redirect the ship that has lost its course.

The Stoics gave a needed response to the challenges of their times. They were original in their form, yet in their teachings they drank from the ancient rivers of wisdom, which flow eternally by our side.

We also need to find responses to the challenges of our times, which are the challenges we are responsible for. Some might say that we cannot truly be Stoic today, just as we cannot truly live like the Romans. It is said that our times require our solutions.

But Stoicism can offer us immense consolation, peace and strength.

And together with other currents of wisdom, adapted to our times, we may find the guiding star that will help us navigate through these turbulent times, into what will perhaps be a new and better world.

Gilad Sommer

# RECOMMENDED BOOKS AND LINKS

ORIGINALS
Marcus Aurelius - Meditations
Seneca – Letters, On the Briefness of Life, On the Happy Life
Epictetus – Enchiridion, Discourses

*In addition to the original writings of the Stoics, there are many good books with commentaries and interpretations.*

The Inner Citadel – Pierre Hadot
*Probably the best book on Marcus Aurelius and the Meditations, and not only, but also on Epictetus and Stoicism as a whole. Highly recommended.*
How to be a Stoic: Using ancient philosophy to live a modern life – Massimo Pigliucci
Stoicism and the Art of Happiness – Donald Robertson
A Guide to the Good Life: The Ancient Art of Stoic Joy – William B. Irvine
Musonius Rufus and Education in the Good Life – J.T. Dillon

TheStoiclife.org (https://sites.google.com/site/thestoiclife/)
*A comprehensive site dedicated to Stoicism as a Way of Life.*

https://howtobeastoic.wordpress.com/
*The wonderful blog of Massimo Pigliucci or as he calls it "an evolving guide to practical Stoicism for the 21st century".*

http://www.krauselabs.net/writings/thesis/
*Stoicism and Historical Action during the Nervan-Antonine Dynasty, from the blog the Faith of a Heretic, Chris Krause. (Extracted, March 2018.)*

http://www.traditionalstoicism.com/
*A blog about Stoic Living, maintained by Chris Fisher.*

New Acropolis International Organization (www.acropolis.org)
An international organization dedicated to the practice of philosophy as a way of life. It also has a large resource of articles on the subject (library.acropolis.org)

The Daily Stoic (https://dailystoic.com/new-start-here/)
A well known site by the writer Ryan Holiday, somewhat commercial yet contains useful information about practicing Stoicism in everyday life.

Modern Stoicism (http://modernstoicism.com/)
A scholarly and well-developed site by the Modern Stoic movement, creators of Stoic Week and the Stoicon.

# IMAGE ATTRIBUTIONS

**Pg. 29 - Diogenes and Alexander**
Wikimedia Commons contributors, "File:Diogenes and Alexander by Lovis Corinth.jpg," *Wikimedia Commons, the free media repository,* https://commons.wikimedia.org/w/index.php?title=File:Diogenes_and_Alexander_by_Lovis_Corinth.jpg&oldid=290989855 (accessed October 18, 2019).

**Pg. 32 - Zeno of Citium**
Wikimedia Commons contributors, "File:Paolo Monti - Servizio fotografico (Napoli, 1969) - BEIC 6353768.jpg," *Wikimedia Commons, the free media repository*, https://commons.wikimedia.org/w/index.php?title=File:Paolo_Monti_-_Servizio_fotografico_(Napoli,_1969)_-_BEIC_6353768.jpg&oldid=263334179 (accessed October 18, 2019).

**Pg 35 - Zeus of Smyrne**
Wikimedia Commons contributors, "File:Jupiter Smyrna Louvre Ma13.jpg," *Wikimedia Commons, the free media repository,* https://commons.wikimedia.org/w/index.php?title=File:Jupiter_Smyrna_Louvre_Ma13.jpg&oldid=336279150 (accessed October 18, 2019).

**Pg. 37 - Chrysippus of Soli**
Wikimedia Commons contributors, "File:Chrysippos BM 1846.jpg," *Wikimedia Commons, the free media repository,* https://commons.wikimedia.org/w/index.php?title=File:Chrysippos_BM_1846.jpg&oldid=362354364 (accessed October 18, 2019).

**Pg. 38 – Panateius**
Wikimedia Commons contributors, "File:Panaetius Nuremberg Chronicle.jpg," *Wikimedia Commons, the free media repository,* https://commons.wikimedia.org/w/index.php?title=File:Panaetius_Nuremberg_Chronicle.jpg&oldid=142130531 (accessed October 18, 2019).

**Pg. 39 - Cicero**
Wikimedia Commons contributors, "File:Cicero.PNG," *Wikimedia Commons, the free media repository,* https://commons.wikimedia.org/w/index.php?title=File:Cicero.PNG&oldid=318805654 (accessed October 18, 2019).

**Pg. 49 - The Double Herm of Socrates and Seneca**
Royal Museums of Berlin, *Description of the ancient sculptures excluding the Pergamon finds,* https://digi.ub.uni-heidelberg.de/diglit/berlin1891/0171/image (accessed October 18, 2019).

**Pg. 50 - Thrasea Paetus**
Wikimedia Commons contributors, "File:Bronnikov Thrasea Paetus.jpg," *Wikimedia Commons, the free media repository,* https://commons.wikimedia.org/w/index.php?title=File:Bronnikov_Thrasea_Paetus.jpg&oldid=338035398 (accessed October 18, 2019).

**Pg. 52 - Marcus Aurelius**
Art Institute of Chicago, *Aureus (Coin) Portraying Emperor Marcus Aurelius,* https://www.artic.edu/artworks/4528/aureus-coin-portraying-emperor-marcus-aurelius (accessed October 18, 2019).

## International Organization New Acropolis

New Acropolis is a worldwide non-profit organization, with centres in over fifty countries.

Established by Professor Jorge Angel Livraga on the foundations of practical philosophy and universal fraternity, New Acropolis is inspired by a fundamental respect for human dignity beyond differences of race, gender, culture, religion or socio-economic status. New Acropolis respects diversity but also tries to transcend it in search of a higher unity through shared universal ethical principles.

At New Acropolis, philosophy is more than just intellectual food for thought. We study philosophy as a means to integrate science, arts, ethics and metaphysics in order to work towards global human development.

This vision is implemented through a wide range of programs that combine practical education with cultural and volunteering activities. New Acropolis also promotes an awareness of current affairs, both locally and globally and focuses on improving the human condition by aligning ourselves with the laws of nature.

To learn more about New Acropolis, visit **www.acropolis.org**